Talking About Mental Health
with Your Child

& Coloring Book

Professional Life Coach, Inc.

Lexington, Kentucky

TALKING ABOUT MENTAL HEALTH WITH YOUR CHILD & COLORING BOOK

Published by Professional Life Coach, Inc.

Copyright © 2021 by Professional Life Coach, Inc.

ISBN 978-0-578-85866-1

Imprint: Independently Published

Printed in the United States of America

Cover design by Olyvia Telfair

For more information:

Professional Life Coach, Inc.

Website: https://www.professionallifecoachinc.com

Email: professionallifecoachinc@gmail.com

CONTENTS

INTRODUCTION

The concept of a mentally healthy child means being able to reach one's full potential, sustain good relationships by displaying appropriate social skills, and resolve problems with minimal support. Mentally healthy children will be able to function well in different settings. Finally, mentally healthy children will become productive citizens that contribute to a better world.

*According to the Center for Disease Control (CDC), 1 in 6 children in the U.S. between the ages of 2-8 had a mental health-related diagnosis. The data assume these children have been diagnosed due to having received some mental health treatment. It is possible that there are many more children who experience mental health-related problems, but have not been diagnosed or been exposed to mental health treatment.

This coloring book provides a creative tool to help and support adults in the life of a child to have "courageous conversations" about mental health topics. Coloring is a fun activity that is commonly used to improve children's fine motor skills. Coloring is used in this book to engage children in a familiar activity while discussing a sensitive topic like mental health. Adults often use coloring as a coping tool in reducing stress and for improving focus. We aim to share mental health topics using practical language that supportive adults may adapt while talking with children.

The primary goal of the book is to normalize mental health topics in the homes of children. The secondary goal is to begin to introduce how talking about thoughts and emotions affects mental health. The third goal is to create opportunities for adults who are important in a child's life to build a more engaged and emotionally connected relationship. The fourth goal is to allow the adult to validate and create a safe space where children will know they are understood and supported if they are experiencing a mental health issue. The final goal is to help adults determine if their child needs professional mental health and to provide possible resources.

*https://www.cdc.gov/childrensmentalhealth/data.html

ABOUT PROFESSIONAL LIFE COACH, INC.

MISSION

Professional Life Coach, Inc. aims to offer mental health resources and programming, consulting, and coaching services to communities. Our services focus on racially diverse families while empowering women.

BOARD OF DIRECTORS

Shambra Mulder, PhD has more than 25 years of experience advocating for those who are considered "the least of these." She is guided by her calling to help people reach their fullest potential. Dr. Mulder combines her gift of discernment, personal life experiences, academic training, and professional experiences to help people make informed and healthy decisions. She earned her degree in School Psychology and a doctorate (Ph.D.) in Educational Psychology. Dr. Mulder holds a certification in School Psychology, where she spent eight years working in the public schools advocating for quality education for students with various disabilities. She also completed an advanced program required for the Director of Special Education certification and an advanced certification in psychotherapy. She is currently a Licensed Psychologist with her practice called Abundant Living Psychological and Coaching Services for Children and Adolescents, PLLC. She has goals of working with children and adolescents from underserved populations. Dr. Mulder commits to several community service organizations and is a Life Member of Sigma Gamma Rho Sorority, Inc.

JoJuana Leavell-Greene retired in 2019 after 33 years in Human Resources, Accounting, Auditing, and Training. She was born in June 1963 in Elkton (Todd County), Kentucky and lived most of her childhood in Hopkinsville and Bowling Green, Kentucky. Leavell-Greene is the Owner/Operator of J, J, V's Order My Steps d/b/a GreeneLandingKY and Nanny's Land, which grows fresh produce sites in food desert areas. She is a Life Member of many organizations including Ruby of Sigma Gamma Rho Sorority, Inc., Kentucky State University Alumni, NAACP, NCNW, ASALH, and Blacks in Government (BIG). Leavell-Greene is the President of the Kentucky Society of Certified Public Managers (KSCPM), Vice-Chair of Board of Directors at Community Ventures (CVC) of Kentucky, Community Outreach Liaison and Treasurer for Lexington-Fayette County NAACP, and a member of Total Grace Baptist Church. She resides in Lexington, Kentucky.

Yolanda Stepp earned her Associate in Art degree at Lexington Community College in 2002. Stepp currently works at Lexington Healthcare System, and is working on her 29th year of service. She is a believer of GOD and what faith can do. Her mission is to help and serve her community. She enjoys helping others when and if she can with her time and labor. During her personal time, she loves watching good movies and family time. She resides in Lexington, Kentucky with her husband and child.

Professional Life Coach, Inc. is a 501c3 nonprofit organization. To contact and/or provide donations can be found on their website: https://www.professionallifecoachinc.com

Coloring Pages
& Mental Health
Content

YOU MATTER: BE SELF-FUL

This lesson is to help you talk with children about their **SELF** development to win in life.

You matter to your parents, friends, and family as much as you must matter to yourself!

You are special, unique, one-of-a-kind, and are the best you on the earth.

What does it mean to win in your life? What does it look like when you are winning?

Some of the ways it means for you to win: be content with what you have, be grateful for what you have, give to others, help others, reach personal and professional goals like grades, earn rewards, have positive relationships/friendships, and what you need and what you want.

The following are five qualities:

SELF-Esteem: You appreciate and are able to accept praise from others when you win.

SELF-Worth: You believe that you are destined to win.

SELF-Confidence: You believe that you can win.

SELF-Love: You do what is needed to win because you deserve to win.

SELF-Efficacy: You know and believe that you can do what it takes to win.

You develop these five qualities of SELF through practicing SELF-awareness and SELF-reflection. Become SELF-aware of who you are and what you have to do to WIN.*

Practice SELF-reflection by looking at your thoughts and behaviors. Ensure that you practice positive and helpful language and behavior reflective of these five qualities. Some of the tools that one uses for SELF-reflection:

1. Journaling to write daily reflections.
2. Displaying positive affirmations on a mirror or wall.
3. Carrying the positive affirmations in the pocket or phone.
4. Vision Boarding positive pictures and words.
5. Surrounding yourself with those who want you to win, feed you positive affirmation, and keep you focused on the path to WIN in life.

Provide the child(ren) with specific examples and allow them to share their personal examples of winning.

MENTAL HEALTH DIAGNOSES

Mental Health Diagnoses aims to discuss symptoms of some of the common mental health disorders experienced by children that may or may not require professional help (by licensed/trained mental health providers). The following information will briefly provide conversation starters that will give a glimpse into some of the thought patterns and behaviors that may exist in children.

1. **Mood Disorders/Depression:**
   Symptoms include sadness, hopelessness, lethargy, excessive sleeping, isolation, crying a lot, anger, bullying, weight gain/loss, inattention or problems concentrating, and loss of interest in favorite activities.

How do you feel? Do you feel sad? What are you looking forward to? Have you been sleeping more or less than you used to? Have you been getting in trouble at school/home more than usual? Do you find yourself crying unexpectedly? Have you stopped doing the fun things you used to enjoy? Would you prefer to be alone or be with your friends/family?

2. **Anxiety-Related Disorder (social anxiety, separation anxiety, panic disorder):**
   Symptoms include irritability, muscle tension, irrational fear, restlessness/fidgetiness, distress during separation from family/home, and fear of judgment/rejection in social situations.

Do you worry about your parents when you are away? Do you avoid being around peers because you think you will be embarrassed or rejected (they won't like you)? Do you have times when your heart races or you sweat, shake, or become light-headed when in new places or doing something tricky like tests?

3. **Stress-Related Disorder/Post Trauma Stress Disorder (PTSD):**
   Provided the child has experienced/witnessed a traumatic event or significant neglect/abuse, the symptoms may include the following: being emotionally withdrawn/numb, inappropriate emotional reactions, recurrent memories of the trauma, nightmares, avoiding certain places/people that remind them of the trauma, hypervigilance/jumpy/startle response or uncharacteristic anger outbursts.

Can we talk about (insert trauma)? Do you remember/think about it a lot? Do you have nightmares or trouble sleeping? Were you afraid that you or someone will get hurt/die? Do you have a problem remembering what happened, or are you confused about anything that happened?

4. **Learning Disorder/School Problems**
   The child is having a lot of problems in school (i.e., getting work completed, difficulty academics, behavior problems, difficulty paying attention in the classroom, or making friends).

What is your favorite subject in school? What don't you like about school? Do you get in trouble in the class/school more than others? Do you have friends in school? Are you being picked on/bullied in school/on the bus? Do you believe your grades/test scores tell what you have learned?

Resource:
Mental health disorders are outlined in the American Psychiatric Association Diagnostic and Statistical Manual of Mental Disorders – Fifth Edition (DSM-V), which is used by mental health professionals.

BUILDING RESILIENCE

Resilience is the ability to come back from a traumatic experience, disappointment, respond to unexpected changes, deal with difficult people/situations, and stay strong during tough times. Resilience is also the ability to learn from those experiences and continue to thrive afterward. It involves adapting to changes and choosing to maintain a positive outlook on life.

For example, after you get a grade lower than expected on a test, you learn what you could have done better, and then prepare to get a better grade on the next test.

The following are ways to help your children gain more resiliency:

1. Help them make stable connections to parents, siblings, peers, and family members. Help them build trust in others who can provide a safe space to share their personal feelings and thoughts. They must have someone who can validate their experiences when something traumatic has occurred in their life.

Identify with the child(ren) the person(s) they should go to if they need to talk to someone:

_____

_____

2. Help them identify extracurricular activities, hobbies, and communities that they may join to provide support, enjoyment, and purpose in life. Encourage participation in mentoring groups, faith-based organizations, and other types of groups that share their interests.

What support group can they join that will be the 'best fit' for their goals and needs?

_____

_____

3. Help them find ways to take care of their minds and bodies. This includes healthy eating, positive behavior, and critical thinking. For example, they may enjoy exercise or doing mindfulness/meditation activities that help them be calm and change their mood/thoughts from negative to positive. This also includes avoiding things that have a negative impact such as harmful tv/social media interactions.

What activities or strategies should they do to help improve their mood and health?

_____

_____

4. Help them find their purpose in life to help them have something to look forward to as they grow up. Create opportunities to volunteer and help others who are more in need. Help them practice forgiveness, practice gratefulness, and take control of improving their life.

What are some goals or things you will do to get better or do better moving forward?

_____

_____

Reference: American Psychological Association: Building your Resilience (2012)
https://www.apa.org/topics/resilience

UNHEALTHY THINKING

Sometimes our brains, thoughts, what we say to ourselves or self-talk (sometimes not aloud) are not right for us. They do not help us make good decisions and often tell us negative things like:

"I am not a good person."
"I can not control my behavior."
"They don't like me."
"I am not smart."
"I am bad."

These thoughts are likely not the most accurate.

Sometimes we make bad choices. **Sometimes** we do bad things. We are not good at **everything**. There **may** be people that treat us as if they do not like us. There are other ways to think about it, and thinking about it in different ways is likely more helpful. For example, "If I believe that I am wrong, I don't try to do good things." Or "If I don't believe that I belong in college, I won't apply."

***Ask the child for some of the thoughts s/he has that are not helpful. You should also share some of the thoughts you have had and how it affected your behavior.

Most of the cognitive distortions are exaggerations or inflexible. Most of them include words like "always, never, no one, should, or I can't." The following are some of the examples of cognitive distortions:

1. Overgeneralization: Make conclusions based on little information.
2. Minimization: Choose to ignore important information.
3. Magnification: Choose to overemphasize or highlight irrelevant information.
4. Personalization: Take responsibility for things that are not under your control.

***Children must be aware of their thoughts and be determined to choose a better thought process.

Resource:
To learn more about Cognitive Behavior Therapy and Cognitive Distortions, study the works of psychiatrists Aaron T. Beck and David D. Burns.

RACE-RELATED STRESS/TRAUMA

Racial trauma is when people experience a large amount of personal stress due to racism. The effects of this stress are related to their mental and physical health. The stress becomes a race-related trauma when there is ongoing exposure to harm when others complete unintentional comments, aggressive acts and are treated unfairly due to the color of their skin. Racial trauma is also experienced by consistently watching others experience racism in daily life through television and social media.
+++

What if your child says something that indicates "self-hate" or feelings of distress like:
"I wish I did not look like I do."
"I wish I was white or had long pretty hair."
"I wish my skin was lighter."

The above statements are likely the results of something a bully said to them at school, something they saw on television or social media, or the recognition that they are treated differently than a peer by a loved one or a teacher. They begin to figure they are different because of their skin color. Research showed that children recognize different races and skin colors at the very young age of three. Adults must be comfortable talking to their children about race. Children can begin to "internalize" and believe these negative things about themselves and their race.

The conversation should be focused on combating "internalized racism" and pushing a positive message about the child's race (called race socialization). Race socialization is the process by which we teach children how to navigate, survive, and interpret messages about race. Sometimes the messages are verbal or taught directly; however, sometimes the messages are learned through observation and media. These messages should:
1. Increase self-pride in their race (Black, African American, Asian American, and Biracial, etc.).
2. Share the reality of racism and racial inequity.
3. Show the child how to interact with others of different races.
4. Teach them not to believe some of the negative messages/stereotypes they encounter about a specific racial group.
5. Encourage the child to speak up when they see or experience racism.

Additional recommendations:
1. Use this opportunity to gather and share examples of positive stories and historical people who look like the child or within their race.
2. Use an example of your personal experience with racism or witness of racism.
3. Remember to be a model of showing the child positive interactions and talk about people of different races.

Additional Resources to Help Parents Address Racism & Discrimination:
https://www.healthychildren.org/English/healthy-living/emotional-wellness/Building-Resilience/Pages/Talking-to-Children-About-Racial-Bias.aspx
The National Child Trauma Stress Network (NCTSN). Cultural Responsiveness to Racial Trauma **https://www.nctsn.org/sites/default/files/resources/special-resource/cultural responsiveness to racial trauma understanding racial trauma why it matters and what to do.pdf**
Gaskin, A. (2015, August). Racial socialization. *CYF News.*
http://www.apa.org/pi/families/resources/newsletter/2015/08/racial-socialization

GRIEF

The acronym DABDA represents Denial, Anger, Bargaining, Depression, and Acceptance.

In the Grief Process it is natural to experience grief when you have experienced a loss such as the death of a family member, loss of a dream, terminal illness, divorce, loss of a friendship, and extreme disappointment. Use the DABDA model to assist children with moving through the stages of the grief process.

Denial   I can't believe _____ is gone.

Anger   I am so mad at _____ or that _____ happened.

Bargaining   I wish it was _____ that would have _____.
                    I would give _____ to make _____ not happen.

Depression   I am sad that _____.
                    I would do _____ to stop this pain.

Acceptance   I am so grateful for the good times I had with _____.
                    I choose to remember the good things about_____.
                    I will honor _____by doing_____.
                    I forgive _____ and myself for_____.

Note that not everyone will experience these stages; some people will move through them in a different order and over time.

Reference: Kübler-Ross, Elisabeth. (1969). *On Death and Dying.* Scribner.

CRISIS

This exercise assists with how to recognize and work through a crisis (an emotional breakdown or a reaction to an unexpected traumatic event). The goal is to calm the child down or decrease the emotional response to trauma.

C – Calm down. Attempt to regulate the emotions so that the child can come to himself/herself.

R – Rational thinking. Ensure that the person is not catastrophizing/overreacting. Clear up cognitive distortions - thoughts that are not helpful and not precisely accurate/verifiable.

I – Identify/share with a support system that can provide more information about the child.

S – Safety needs to be accessed and secured (ensure the child is not going to harm himself/herself or others).

I – Introduce fundamental coping mechanisms for future use, such as meditation and breathing techniques (Example: Count from 1 to 10).

S – Seek and share mental health resources (process events and assess suicidal/homicidal thoughts).

Reference:

Minnesota National Alliance on Mental Illness (NAMI): Mental Health Crisis Planning for Children Learn to Recognize, Manage, Prevent and Plan for Your Child's Mental Health Crisis

http://childcrisisresponsemn.org/wp-content/uploads/2012/01/KidsCrisisBooklet10.25.10.pdf

PROCESSING TRAUMA

Children must be given the opportunity and space to discuss and process traumatic experiences. Use this time to correct faulty or negative thinking such as they were at fault, will be punished, are a bad person, or have fears about their safety.

It is also important for parents and adults to recognize changes in the child's mood and behavior. For example, is the child sleeping more, isolated in their room away from family/friends, angry, and displaying acting out behaviors like fighting?

You may ask if others have witnessed changes in the child's behavior or think to determine if professional help is needed.

Adverse Childhood Experience (ACE) – indicates there are life-long negative effects after a child has experienced a traumatic event. The Center for Disease Control (CDC) and Kaiser Permanente Organization conducted the Adverse Childhood Experiences (ACE) Study between 1995-1997 using an "ACE Survey" to investigate whether a child has experienced one of the following childhood traumatic experiences:

- Abuse
  - **Emotional abuse:** A parent, stepparent, or adult living in your home swore at you, insulted you, put you down, or acted in a way that made you afraid that you might be physically harmed.
  - **Physical abuse:** A parent, stepparent, or adult living in your home pushed, grabbed, slapped, threw something at you, or hit you so hard that you had marks or were injured.
  - **Sexual abuse:** An adult, relative, family friend, or stranger who was at least five years older than you ever touched or fondled your body in a sexual way, made you sexually touch his/her body, or attempted to have sexual intercourse with you.
- Household Challenges
  - **Mother treated violently:** Your mother or stepmother was pushed, grabbed, slapped, had something thrown at her, kicked, bitten, hit with a fist, hit with something hard, repeatedly hit for over at least a few minutes, or ever threatened or hurt by a knife or gun by your father (or stepfather) or mother's boyfriend.
  - **Substance abuse in the household:** A household member was a problem drinker or alcoholic, or used street drugs.
  - **Mental illness in the household:** A household member was depressed, mentally ill, or attempted suicide.
  - **Parental separation or divorce:** Your parents were ever separated or divorced.
  - **Incarcerated household member:** A household member went to jail or prison.
- Neglect
  - **Emotional neglect:** Someone in your family helped you feel important or special, you felt loved, people in your family looked out for each other and felt close to each other, and your family was a source of strength and support.[2]
  - **Physical neglect:** There was someone to take care of you, protect you, and take you to the doctor if you needed it[2], you didn't have enough to eat, your parents were too drunk or too high to take care of you, and you had to wear dirty clothes.

In addition to the traumatic experiences described above, many children are exposed to trauma through media or witness violence in their homes or community. It may or may not include losing a family member, classmate, and friends dying by gun violence. When asking children about whether they experienced one or more of these types of trauma, notice the study concluded that those who experienced four or more of them have the most harmful effects in life including substance abuse, premature death, heart disease, mental health conditions, etc.

For more information about trauma and to obtain a copy of the ACE Survey: https://www.cdc.gov/violenceprevention/aces/index.html
About the CDC-Kaiser ACE Study |Violence Prevention|Injury .... https://www.cdc.gov/violenceprevention/aces/about.html

SUICIDE ASSESSMENT

I. Assess suicidal ideation by asking the questions:
Have you ever wanted to die? Have you ever thought about what it would be like if you were not alive anymore? Have you ever thought about hurting yourself?

Asking these questions have been shown to prevent suicide. Suicidal ideation is common and doesn't always lead to suicidal behavior/attempts. However, if the answer is "Yes" move on to the other questions.

II. Assess whether they have access to means to hurt themselves:
If you were to hurt yourself, how would you do it?

May have to share with others so that they can limit their access.

III. Assess prior attempts:
Have you ever tried to end your life or hurt yourself before?

Prior behavior is the best predictor of future behavior.

IV. Assess protective factors that would prevent them from hurting themselves:
What would make you not want to hurt yourself?
What can I do to help you so that you won't hurt yourself?

It is vital that you share their positive attributes, importance, life purpose, and other positive reasons for living.

V. Ensure safety and create a safety plan if necessary.
VI. Can we develop a written plan that you would agree to use if you ever want to hurt yourself or end your life?

*Share or call the Suicide Hotline (1-800-273-TALK/8255). Call 911. Alert parents.
Connect them to other community resources (counselors, support systems, pastor, etc.)*

Resources:

National Suicide Prevention Lifeline https://suicidepreventionlifeline.org/
The Lifeline provides 24/7, free and confidential support for people in distress, prevention and crisis resources for you or your loved ones, and best practices for professionals.

Columbia University Lighthouse Project's – Columbia Protocol — also known as the Columbia-Suicide Severity Rating Scale (C-SSRS)
https://cssrs.columbia.edu/wp-content/uploads/Community-Card-Parents-2020.pdf

WHAT TO EXPECT IN THERAPY

What are some significant reasons to seek professional help or mental health therapy?:

1. Begin to recognize changes in a child's behavior in at least two settings (home and school/daycare) that are uncharacteristic. The changes may be in their display of externalizing or outward behaviors (i.e. fighting, yelling, excessive emotional responses) or internalizing or inward behaviors (i.e. withdrawal/isolation, problems with sleeping or eating, sadness).
2. Aware that the child has experienced a trauma (any situation that caused a big change in their life/thoughts) that was unexpected and uncommon to their peers. Common traumatic experiences include loss of loved ones, serious sickness, divorce, and bullying.
3. The child engages in dangerous behaviors or expresses harmful thoughts. Dangerous behaviors include self-harming like cutting, connecting with adults on the internet, promiscuity, and smoking marijuana. Harmful thoughts include suicidal thoughts ("I wish I was dead.") or homicidal thoughts ("I will kill you.")

How do I find a therapist that will be a good fit for my child and family?

1. Request a referral from your pediatrician/doctor or school counselor.
2. Search online directories.
3. Ask other parents, family, and friends.
4. Call your health insurance provider; they will be able to identify therapists who accept your insurance.

What do you do after choosing a therapist(s) that might be a good fit?

1. Make an initial call to the therapist's office or complete online intake forms. Ask if they are accepting clients, accept your insurance (if applicable), and whether they do an initial consultation.
2. Talk with the child about seeing a therapist or someone that can help them. You might express your concerns and goals for therapy. Ask the child their thoughts and possible changes they would like to make with a therapist's help.

***Caution: acknowledge the child's hesitation, but consider continuing to the initial visit to allow the therapist to address concerns.

What to expect at the initial visit/consultation with the therapist?

1. Be prepared to answer key questions on the visit. Some potential questions that the therapist may ask: 1) Reasons you are seeking therapy or what are your concerns; 2) Explain your expectations for therapy or what would be some potential goals; 3) Determine what success would look like; 4) Explain the child's support system or home/school environments; 5) Identify any barriers to treatment goals.
2. Be prepared to ask questions of the therapist. Some potential questions related to: 1) potential assessments; 2) timeline for diagnosis and treatment goals; 3) Costs/co-pays; 4) parent participation; 5) desire for regular updates on treatment progress.

Other important information:

1. Confidentiality is very important. The legal reasons to disregard confidentiality is if the child expresses suicidal thoughts, homicidal thoughts, or is being harmed. Police, hospitalization, and reports to child protective services may be involved.
2. In the case of minors (under 18 years old), the parent is the "legal" client. Parents have access to all clinical records and must provide/remove consent for treatment.
3. If you are not satisfied with the treatment and/or the therapist is not a good fit, please consider expressing concern with the therapist before stopping services. If you decide to end treatment, the therapist may refer the child to another provider and prepare the child for the end of services.

RESOURCES

Finding a mental health provider:

Access an online directory of mental health providers.
Contact your medical insurance company to request providers that accept your insurance.
Access your Community Mental Health Center that may accept a sliding pay scale.
Contact your school counselor/district student support services.

Emergency Response:

• Call 911 (especially if safety is compromised)
• Report to any Hospital Emergency Room
• State Mental Health Hospital
• Call National Suicide Prevention Lifeline
• Call National Domestic Violence Hotline

If abuse or neglect is suspected:

• Call Child Protective Services in your local area.

For more information about mental health topics:

• National Alliance on Mental Illness (NAMI)
• Mental Health America (MHA)
• The Association of Black Psychologists (ABPsi)
• American Psychological Association (APA)
• American Psychiatric Association (APA)
• National Association of School Psychologists (NASP)
• Substance Abuse and Mental Health Services Administration (SAMHSA)
• National Child Traumatic Stress Network (NCTSN)

Additional resources available in your local area/state:

• State Psychological Association
• Local area university counseling/psychology/psychiatric services
• State Department for Behavioral Health

Made in the USA
Columbia, SC
11 August 2023

21504326R00015